FORMAC P

CANADA'S ATLANTIC
SEASHORE

A visual guide to starfish, shellfish, seashells,
plants, insects, birds and more!

Written and illustrated by Jeffrey C. Domm

Formac Publishing Company Limited
Halifax, Nova Scotia

Formac Publishing Company Limited recognizes the support of the Province of Nova Scotia through the Department of Communities, Culture and Heritage. We are pleased to work in partnership with the Culture Division to develop and promote our culture resources for all Nova Scotians. We acknowledge the financial support of the Government of Canada through the Canada Book Fund for our publishing activities. We acknowledge the support of the Canada Council for the Arts which last year invested $20.1 million in writing and publishing throughout Canada.

The Canada Council | Le Conseil des Arts
for the Arts | du Canada

NOVA SCOTIA
Tourism, Culture and Heritage

Library and Archives Canada Cataloguing in Publication

Domm, Jeffrey C., 1958-
    Formac pocketguide to Canada's Atlantic seashore : a visual guide to starfish, shellfish, seashells, plants, insects, birds and more! / written & illustrated by Jeffrey C. Domm. -- 2nd ed.

Includes index.
Issued also in an electronic format.
ISBN 978-1-4595-0064-8

    1. Seashore biology--Atlantic Coast (Canada)--Guidebooks.
2. Seashore animals--Atlantic Coast (Canada)--Identification.
3. Seashore plants--Atlantic Coast (Canada)--Identification.
I. Title. II. Title: Canada's Atlantic seashore.

QH95.7.D65 2012   578.769'9091634   C2012-900013-2

Formac Publishing Company Limited
5502 Atlantic Street
Halifax, Nova Scotia
B3H 1G4
www.formac.ca

Printed and bound in Korea.

Contents

Exploring the Seashore

Standing at the edge of the sea is exhilarating. This is the meeting place of terrestrial and marine life, where two ecosystems intertwine. As wading birds scurry in the surf, the salty wind and the sound of the breakers overwhelm your senses, and you wonder how delicate creatures thrive in this turbulent environment.

On the beach you see dried seaweed and fragments of shells. Gulls and sandpipers feed at the water's edge, and effortlessly take wing as you approach.

The rocks are slippery with algae but you find footing on the rough barnacles. In a tidal pool you take a careful look to see what might be moving among the rocks, shells and weeds. It's low tide; below you are fronds of seaweed, cemented to the rock by their holdfasts. They are still moist from the water that sustains them and covered with microscopic life. Seaweed, the 'forest' of the ocean, provides protection for larger animals as well as for a host of smaller organisms. As the tide rises, the fronds flow gently back and forth in the waves.

The incessant movement of water due to wind, currents and tides is integral to this environment. Marine plants and animals have adapted to the inundating water. For example, whelks, barnacles, mussels and limpets, fastened to the rocky surfaces, have hard shells that protect their flesh from predators and also act as a defense against the waves. The water also carries in rich supplies of plankton and dead plants and animals that nourish other organisms, such as starfish, anemones and crabs.

SEASHORE ZONES

Seashores differ dramatically around the world but on any given continent you can find variations of either large boulders, mud flats, sandy beaches, or small pebbles and rocks. On Canada's Atlantic coast you can find all of these habitats, and they all have one thing in common: the intertidal zone which lies between the high and low tide marks.

The upper region of the beach, above the high water mark, is called the spray or dry land zone, and very little salt water reaches here. There might be footprints of a raccoon or gulls in search of food, and some periwinkles, snails or barnacles attached to the rocks.

As you walk towards the ocean during low tide you come upon small pools of salt water left behind during high tide where more snails and mussels are clinging to rocks. And closer still, the mid-tide zone may be populated with birds feeding on small molluscs and worms that burrow into the sand.

The liveliest area of the shore is the low-tide zone, covered by water except when the tide is unusually low. It is teeming with crabs, sea urchins, starfish, seaweed and even small fish.

Low tide is a very good time to start observing life on

the seashore. If you visit the same beach over an extended period of days or weeks you will notice how the tides affect the life of the beach. You will appreciate how the world at your feet depends on powerful forces — the rotation of the earth, the wind that is set in motion by the sun, and the tides that are carried by the gravitational pull of the moon and the sun.

TIDES

The most familiar tidal pattern is the twice-daily alternation of high and low tides. Each high and each low occurs every twelve hours and twenty-five minutes, so that every day the low tide occurs 50 minutes later. You can consult tide tables available from the Canadian Hydrographic Service, under the Department of Fisheries and Oceans (website: http://www.lau.chs-shc.dfo-mpo.gc.ca/english/Canada.shtml) and also from most local tourist bureaus. The tables predict the time of high and low tides for a particular area on any given date.

Twice a month, when the sun and moon are aligned relative to the Earth, the combined gravitational pull results in the largest range of tides, called spring tides. The distance between the high water

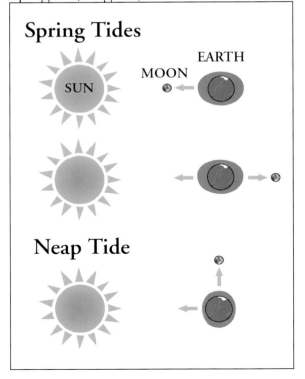

6

and low water is greatest at this time. When the sun and moon lie at right angles to the earth (also twice a month), the difference between the high tide and the low tide is significantly smaller. This smaller range is called the neap tide.

There are areas where the tides are less regular, and there are also variations in tidal heights from one area to another. In Atlantic Canada, on the shores of the Bay of Fundy, you can see some of the most spectacular tides in the world. As the water is funnelled into the broad mouth of the bay, it stacks up on itself pushing into the narrower, shallower areas at the head of the bay. This results in an extreme variation between high and low tide. In places along the shores of Minas Basin the tide comes in over the vast expanse of mud flats at great speed, faster than you can run.

TIPS FOR BEACHCOMBING

The power of the sea is not to be underestimated, even when you are on dry land. When appreciating the magnificent beauty and abundance of life forms on the beach, it is a good idea to be well prepared. Find out about the tides on the beach you want to visit and make sure that you see how quickly the water is coming in. On a rocky shore, when the surf is high, stay a safe distance back from the breakers.

On a beach trip, a pair of binoculars is indispensable, and to observe smaller creatures up close you will need a magnifying glass. For your own comfort and protection, wear shoes that give you good footing on the rocks — ones that you don't mind getting wet. You should never go to the shore without a hat and a warm sweater or jacket: even on a bright summer's day, the sea fog may put a chill in the air if the wind is blowing off the sea. At the same time, the glare from the water makes sunglasses a great help and sunscreen essential.

USING THIS BOOK
The contents of this book will introduce you to some of the animals, insects, birds and plants that live in coastal areas. Whether you are strolling along a sandy beach, clambering over rocks, or squishing through mud flats, the first important thing to recognize is the state of the tide. Is it high, low or in between? Once you know which tidal zone you are in, you can identify which habitat corresponds with this beach.

The following icons identify the kinds of beaches and shorelines you will encounter in Atlantic Canada. Some species are found in only one habitat, some in several.

HABITAT

 Rocky Shore

 Sand Shore

 Pebble Shore

 Gravel or Coarse Sand Shore

 Mud Flat

 Salt Marsh

 Fresh Water

 Wharfs or other wooden structures

ZONES

 The Dry land Zone is beyond the reach of the highest tides. A variety of birds nest in this area and flowering plants flourish here.

 The Mid-tide Zone is underwater part of the day. Tidal pools are found in this zone and terrestrial animals can come to this area to feed on marine life.

 The Low-tide Zone is washed by surf when it is not under water. Seaweed and shellfish, such as mussels, that can survive some exposure to wind and sun, can be found in this zone.

SIZE
The size given for each species is based on that of a full-grown, mature individual.

MAGNIFYING GLASS

 These species are best observed with a magnifying glass.

All of these icons and the information in the pages that follow are aids to identifying the life forms around the shore. When comparing what you see with the book, be aware that size and colour vary. Take notes, take photographs, but don't take anything away from its habitat.

Atlantic Rock Crab

- Runs sideways
- Found hiding in low tides under rocks and in crevices
- Raises pincers in defense when approached

1 Front of shell is rounded, smooth

2 10 legs, first 2 are pincers

3 Small eyes in sockets

15 cm / 5.25 in

HABITAT	ZONE	STATUS
		Common

Jonah Crab

- Usually found in seaweed at low tide
- Not very aggressive, so handling is easy

1 Fan-shaped, rounder than Rock Crab

2 Stout pincers with sharp spine near joint

3 10 legs in total, first 2 with pincers

DID YOU KNOW?
Jonah Crab populations are very widespread, stretching from Nova Scotia to Florida and Bermuda.

16 cm / 6.25 in

HABITAT	ZONE	STATUS
		Common

11

Lady Crab

- Rearmost legs have paddle-like ends
- Very aggressive and will pinch with sharp pincers
- Usually found near low tide limit

8 cm / 3 in

HABITAT	ZONE	STATUS
		Common

Green Crab

- Found in tidal pools, among seaweed and under rocks
- Underside is yellow on males, orange-red on females

8 cm / 3 in

HABITAT	ZONE	STATUS
		Common

Acadian Hermit Crab

- Lives in abandoned snail shells
- Found hidden in tidal pools and just below low tide limit

1 Orange pincers with reddish-orange stripe down middle

2 Right pincer is larger

3 Eyes on long, blue eyestalks

DID YOU KNOW?
This crab changes shells as it increases in size, preferring whelk or moon snail shells.

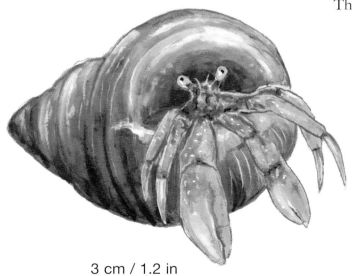

3 cm / 1.2 in

HABITAT   ZONE   STATUS
                                Common

Northern Lobster

- Very occasionally found in tidal pools usually after strong storm surges
- Lifts pincers in defense

1 One pincer is usually larger and blunter, with rounded teeth

2 Pointed beak, 2 short antennae, followed by 2 longer antennae

3 Tail fans at the end

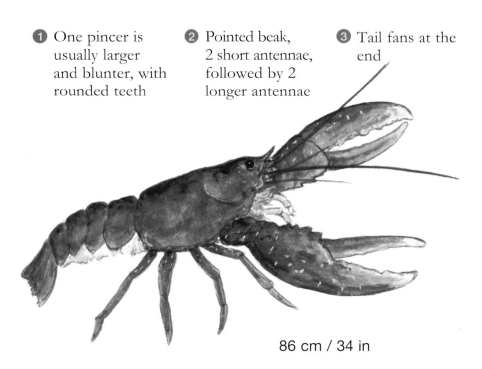

86 cm / 34 in

DID YOU KNOW?

The heavier pincer serves to crush, while the sharper pincer is used to cut prey, such as snails and clams.

HABITAT

ZONE

STATUS
Common

Anemone Sea Spider

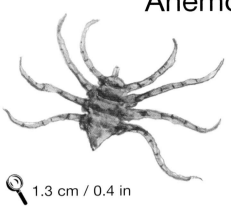

- Small and spider-like, with 8 legs
- Cream coloured or darker, to reddish-brown
- Found among sea anemones

1.3 cm / 0.4 in

HABITAT ZONE

Red Chiton

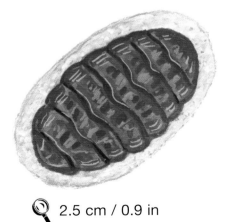

- Feeds on algae on rocks
- Flexible plates permit squeezing between rocks
- Breathes with gills, like a fish

2.5 cm / 0.9 in

HABITAT ZONE

15

Kelp Sowbug

- Crawls along ocean floor
- Colour may be black, reddish-brown, or white, depending on diet

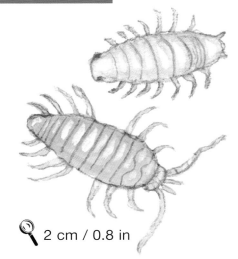

2 cm / 0.8 in

HABITAT   ZONE

Sideswimmer (Scud)

- Very small, light-coloured body, with many legs
- Often seen darting among rocks and seaweed in tidal pools

2 cm / 0.8 in

HABITAT   ZONE

Mysid Shrimp

- Elongated, translucent shrimp-like body
- Can be seen among seaweed and under rocks

2.5 cm / 0.9 in

HABITAT    ZONE

Skeleton Shrimp

- Tiny and light-coloured, with wide legs and hooked claws
- Often found inching along in clumps of seaweed

2 cm / 0.8 in

HABITAT  ZONE

17

Horned Krill Shrimp

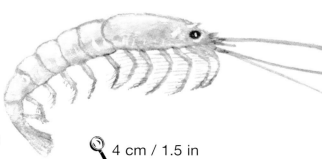

- Elongated, translucent body, looks like a shrimp with a small horn behind head
- Sometimes so abundant offshore that the water looks red

4 cm / 1.5 in

HABITAT

   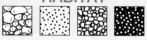

ZONE

Northern Rock Barnacle

- Found in great numbers covering rocks
- Mouth at top is closed during low tides

4 cm / 1.5 in

HABITAT

ZONE

Northern Sea Star

- Slow moving
- Usually found in tidal pools, searching for shelter

1 5 long arms with 4 rows of suckers on underside

2 Usually rosy but occasionally orange, tan, greenish among other colours

3 Covered with short blunt spines

8 cm / 3.25 in

DID YOU KNOW?
This common sea star is often found near mussel beds.

HABITAT	ZONE	STATUS
		Common

19

Purple Sea Star

- Moves slowly
- Found in tidal pools or on wharfs at low tide
- Rare to find a full grown one along the shore, as they move to deeper waters

1 Name is misleading — usually yellow, olive or red-brown

2 Lighter on underside

3 Smooth overall with small blunt spines

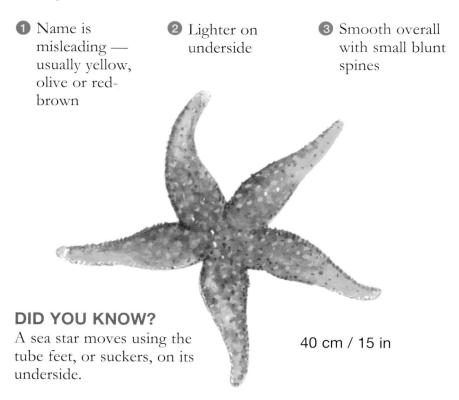

DID YOU KNOW?
A sea star moves using the tube feet, or suckers, on its underside.

40 cm / 15 in

HABITAT	ZONE	STATUS
		Common

20

10 cm / 4 in

Blood Star

• Blood-red colour, occasionally rose, purple, yellow, white, or orange
• Slow moving

HABITAT	ZONE	STATUS
		Common

Daisy Brittle Star

8 cm / 3 in

• Arms wave constantly
• Usually curled up under rocks and pieces of wood in tidal pools

HABITAT	ZONE	STATUS
		Common

30 cm / 12 in

Purple Sunstar

• 7 to 13 arms, thick at their base
• Occasionally caught in tidal pools but mainly seen just off shore

HABITAT	ZONE	STATUS
		Common

Lion's Mane Jellyfish

- Floats near surface
- Often found washed up on sandy beaches at low tide

1 Over 150 tentacles hanging from 8 lobes

2 Saucer-shaped bell of translucent blue, yellow, and brown

3 Colour varies depending on age

2 4 ribbon-like gonads under bell

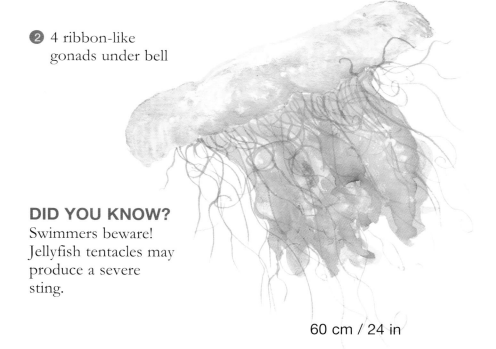

DID YOU KNOW?
Swimmers beware! Jellyfish tentacles may produce a severe sting.

60 cm / 24 in

HABITAT	ZONE	STATUS
		Common

Moon Jellyfish

- Floats near surface by shore and found washed up at low tides
- Sting may cause itch and rash when stepped on

20 cm / 8 in

HABITAT **ZONE**

Sea Gooseberry

5 cm / 2 in

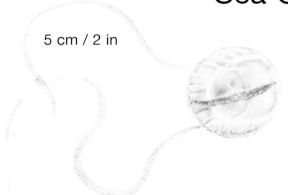

- Floats just below surface of water close to shore
- Very small round transparent bell with long tentacles

HABITAT **ZONE**

Northern Comb Jelly

- Transparent and iridescent
- Found in shallow waters

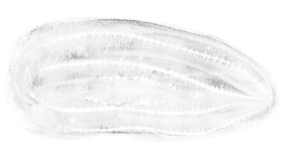

5 cm / 2 in

HABITAT   ZONE

Beroe's Comb Jelly

- Oval shaped with flattened back
- Seen mostly on calm sunny days

11 cm / 5 in

HABITAT   ZONE

Orange-footed Cucumber

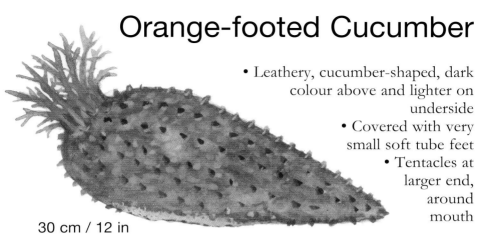

- Leathery, cucumber-shaped, dark colour above and lighter on underside
- Covered with very small soft tube feet
- Tentacles at larger end, around mouth

30 cm / 12 in

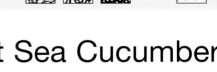

HABITAT ZONE

Scarlet Sea Cucumber

- Round disc off main body, topped with branched red tentacles
- 3 bands of suckers on underside

20 cm / 8 in

HABITAT ZONE

Sand Collar

- Made of a mixture of mucus and sand in which thousands of Moon Snail eggs are buried
- Found in tide pools and on sandy shores

5 cm / 2 in

HABITAT   **ZONE**

Skate Egg Sac

- Bladder with hooked tentacles which attach to aquatic plants
- Occasionally washes to shore once embryo has left the sac

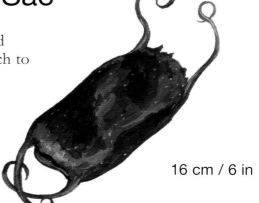

16 cm / 6 in

HABITAT   **ZONE**

Frilled Anemone

- Thick round base with clusters of tentacles at top
- Soft and smooth
- Yellow, red and occasionally mottled

10 cm / 4 in

Northern Red Anemone

- Short red tentacles with white rings
- Attaches to rocks in tide pools, often among seaweed

6 cm / 2.4 in

Silver-spotted Anemone

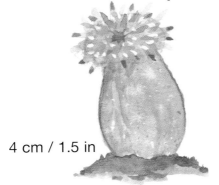

- Short grey tentacles with white pattern
- Attaches to rocks in tidal pools

4 cm / 1.5 in

Eyed Finger Sponge

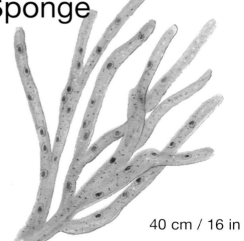

- Colony of finger-like branches
- Dull yellow or grey, bleaches to white out of water
- Branches have small holes, or "eyes"

40 cm / 16 in

HABITAT   ZONE

Organ Pipe Sponge

- Clusters of small, white or yellowish vase-like tubes
- Grows in colonies
- Bush-like, branches connected at the base

1.5 cm / 0.5 in

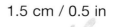

HABITAT   ZONE

28

Red Beard Sponge

20 cm / 8 in

- Orange or red, depending on light, and bleaching to light brown
- Small, thick cluster of thick branches growing in still waters

Palmate Sponge

40 cm / 16 in

- Grows in colonies
- Yellow or red branches are erect and finger-like
- Also called Mermaid's Glove due to its shape

Vase Sponge

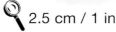 2.5 cm / 1 in

- Vase-like tubes grow on rocks in small colonies
- White or pale brown in colour

Common Periwinkle

- Found in large numbers, covering rocks
- At low tide, secured tightly to rocks, until covered by ebb tide

 2.5 cm / 1 in

HABITAT	ZONE	STATUS
		Common

Rough Periwinkle

- Feeds on algae on rocks at low tide
- Found in large numbers, together with other species of periwinkles

1.2 cm / 0.5 in

HABITAT	ZONE	STATUS
		Common

Smooth Periwinkle

- Usually found among tangles of seaweed
- Eggs, laid in large quantities, can be seen among the periwinkles

 1.3 cm / 0.6 in

HABITAT	ZONE	STATUS
		Common

Northern Moon Snail

- Seen at night at low tide
- Leaves a trail when moving through sand
- Egg sacs often are seen along shoreline (see Sand Collar, page 26)

11 cm / 4.25 in

HABITAT	ZONE	STATUS
		Common

31

Common Northern Whelk

- Juveniles found only in tidal pools.
- Larger, older individuals in deeper water

1 Exterior is chalky grey, yellowish or light hazel, lighter towards tip

2 Large thick shell, white interior

3 Snail is mottled, milky white with black

10 cm / 4 in

HABITAT

ZONE

STATUS
Common

Chink Shell

- Light brown shell with darker bands
- Grey and brown flesh

 1 cm / 0.4 in

Mud Snail

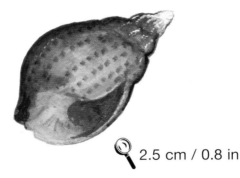

- Reddish-brown to black shell
- Snail has pale grey flesh with hints of black

2.5 cm / 0.8 in

Northern Rosy Margarite

- Rosy pearl colour spiral shaped shell
- Pale grey snail

2 cm / 0.75 in

Swamp Hydrobia

- Smooth, glossy shell
- Snail is dark grey in colour

4 mm / 0.2 in

HABITAT   ZONE

Salt-marsh Snail

1 cm / 0.4 in

- Very thin, smooth shell occasionally with darker bands
- Dark flesh with black foot

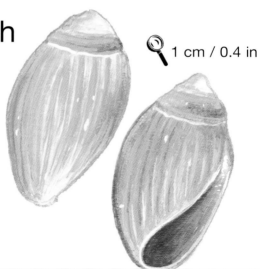

HABITAT   ZONE   STATUS
Common

Sand Dollar

• Washes up on shore at low tide
• Lives in both shallow and deep water

1 Very flat round shell

2 Reddish-brown, darker on upper side

3 Usually greyish-white when bleached

DID YOU KNOW?
Sand dollars make up part of the diet of many ground fish, including cod, haddock and flounder.

8 cm / 3 in

HABITAT	ZONE	STATUS
		Common

Green Sea Urchin

- Clings to rocks, wharfs and seaweed
- Abundant colonies living just off shore

1 Live urchin's spines protect it from predators

2 Empty shell usually found without spines

3 Pores run down the shell

9 cm / 3.9 in

DID YOU KNOW?

Sea urchins are a food source for many fish, including cod and haddock, as well as sea stars and lobster.

HABITAT	ZONE	STATUS
		Common

Blue Mussel

- Attaches to rocks and wooden structures
- Found at low tide in large groups

1 Overall dark bluish exterior with bluish-white inside

2 Filament, called a beard, is used for attaching to rocks

DID YOU KNOW?
The Blue Mussel is a popular edible shellfish that is now farmed in Atlantic Canada.

10.2 cm / 4 in

HABITAT	ZONE	STATUS
		Common

37

Northern Horse Mussel

- Lives offshore, but shells wash up on shore with kelp

❶ Large, heavy, wing-shaped shell

❷ Smooth, with occasional ridge

❸ Grey interior

DID YOU KNOW?
This species is commonly used as fish bait.

22.9 cm / 9 in

HABITAT

ZONE

STATUS
Common

Sea Scallop

- Live scallops found just under the sand
- Propel themselves through water by clapping their shells, releasing a sheet of water

1 Shell convex with ribs leading out in fan-like shape

2 Exterior dark brown at base, fading to reddish-brown at edges

3 Upper valve is reddish brown, lower is cream coloured

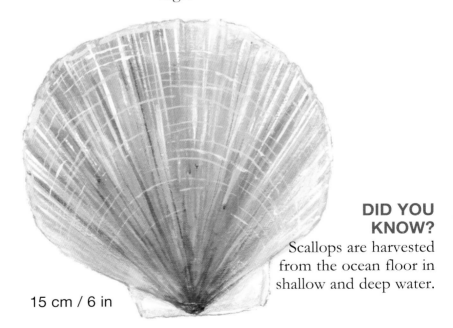

15 cm / 6 in

DID YOU KNOW?

Scallops are harvested from the ocean floor in shallow and deep water.

HABITAT	ZONE	STATUS
		Common

Eastern Oyster

- Live on hard or soft sea floor, close to shore
- Shells often wash up on shore

1 Very large, rough irregular shell

2 Yellow or grey exterior with plated growth ridges

3 Interior of shell milky white with purple near hinge

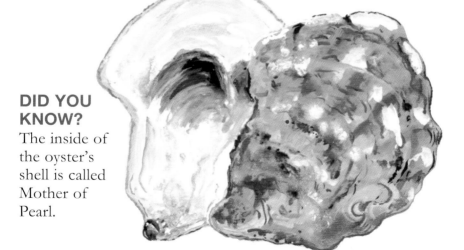

DID YOU KNOW?
The inside of the oyster's shell is called Mother of Pearl.

20 cm / 8 in

HABITAT

ZONE

STATUS
Common

40

Northern Quahog

- Usually find shells washed up on shore
- Animals live in intertidal flats to depths of 15 m (50 feet)

① Extremely thick, broad, oval shell with toothed edge

② Exterior greyish-yellow with brown patterns

③ Interior of shell milky-white with purple stain

11 cm / 4.25 in

DID YOU KNOW?
"Quahog," an Algonquin term, traditionally referred to both the food and the shell, once used as a cutting tool or cup.

HABITAT	ZONE	STATUS
		Common

Atlantic Surf Clam

- Clams found just under the surface of sand or mud
- Shells often wash up on shore

1 Brownish-grey shell with cream-coloured bands

2 Exterior of hinge area is cream-coloured

3 Interior of shell is light cream

DID YOU KNOW?

To escape their predators, Surf Clams can use their foot to "jump" to safety.

15 cm / 6 in

HABITAT

ZONE

STATUS
Common

Common Razor Clam

- Lives just under the surface of sand or gravel beaches
  - Shells wash up on shore

1 Overall shape resembles an old-fashioned razor

2 Elongated, thin shell, roughly 6 times longer than width

3 Interior milky blue

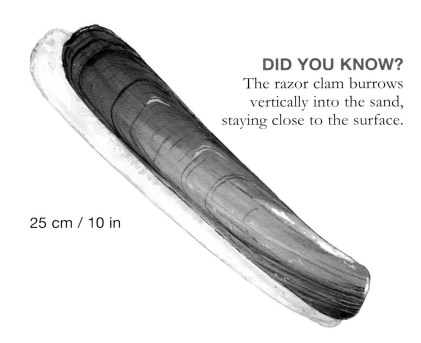

DID YOU KNOW?
The razor clam burrows vertically into the sand, staying close to the surface.

25 cm / 10 in

HABITAT	ZONE	STATUS
		Common

Soft-shelled Clam

- Lives in the sand buried up to 20 cm deep
- Found in fresh-water inlets

1 Very thin, chalky shell

2 Overall milky-white with reddish-brown patterns

3 Interior milky-white with translucent blues and pinks

DID YOU KNOW?
Holes in the sand are made by the clams' siphons. They spurt water when you step close to a hole.

9 cm / 3.5 in

HABITAT	ZONE	STATUS
		Common

Arctic Wedge Clam

- Oval shell is chalky-grey tapering to cream-coloured rounded point
- Deeply cupped inside is milky white, yellow at edges

4 cm / 1.5 in

Macoma Clam

- Smooth, thin, white shell with blue or yellow patterns
- Interior of shell is milky-white with hints of pink

4 cm / 1.5 in

Stimpson Surf Clam

- Lives just below surface with shell exposed during tidal movements
- Yellow-white shell is oval with round, creamy coloured point at hinge end

15 cm / 6 in

Iceland Scallop

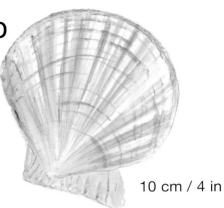

- Convex grey and reddish-brown shell has creamy lines, giving fan-like appearance
- Chalky interior
- Wing on one side of hinge

10 cm / 4 in

Northern Cardita

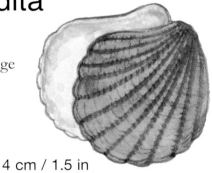

- Fan-like oval shell with ridges leading to outer edge
- Shell is thick grey with interior milky white

4 cm / 1.5 in

Yoldia

- Elongated wedge-shaped white or green shell with brown and blue tints
- Interior of shell is milky-white with blue tints

6 cm / 2.5 in

Cup-and-saucer Limpet

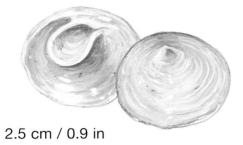

- Usually found attached to rocks or piers at low tide
- Attaches firmly when tide is out

2.5 cm / 0.9 in

Atlantic Slipper Shell

- Usually found in groups, attached to rocks, or on the backs of large shells
- Inside resembles a slipper with toe cap

6.4 cm / 2.5 in

White Limpet

- Usually attached to rocks and shells, along with other limpet species
- Flat compared to other limpets

3 cm / 1.2 in

Green Thread Seaweed

- Stiff, beaded cords
- Grows in clusters in shallow waters
- Disc at base is called a holdfast

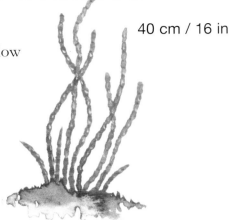

40 cm / 16 in

HABITAT	ZONE	TYPE
	〰〰	Green

Green Rope Seaweed

- Feathery green filaments are beaded and twisted like rope
- Filaments twist together at the holdfast where it attaches to rocks

15 cm / 6 in

HABITAT	ZONE	TYPE
	〰〰	Green

Hollow Green Weed

30 cm / 12 in

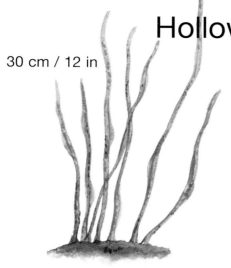

- Tubular, hollow leaves
- Bubbles are seen inside tubes
- Also known as Green Tube Weed

HABITAT	ZONE	TYPE
		Green

Sea Lettuce

- Slippery leaf with holdfast at base
- Pale green turns white at ruffled edges

30 cm / 12 in

HABITAT	ZONE	TYPE
		Green

Horsetail Kelp

- Numerous tentacles
- Brown to olive in colour
- Grows in dense groups on sea floor

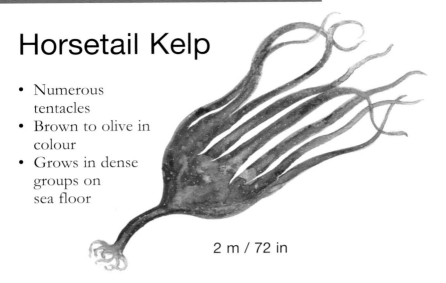

2 m / 72 in

HABITAT	ZONE	TYPE
		Brown

Oar Kelp

- Long, broad leaf
- Olive and yellow in colour
- Collects on shore in large piles which offer shelter to many other seashore creatures

3 m / 9 ft

HABITAT	ZONE	TYPE
		Brown

50

Bladder Wrack

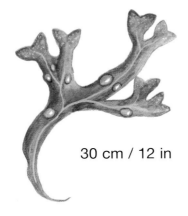

- Very flat with bladders running along branches
- Cemented to rocks by holdfast

30 cm / 12 in

HABITAT	ZONE	TYPE
		Brown

Toothed Wrack

40 cm / 16 in

- Extremely flat, bladderless leaves with deeply toothed edges
- Reproductive ends of plant slightly inflated, tapering to point

HABITAT	ZONE	TYPE
		Brown

Knotted Wrack

- Olive-green or brown with flat branches
- Many bladders on stems and branches
- Often find bush red algae attached

30 cm / 12 in

HABITAT	ZONE	TYPE
		Brown

Sea Sorrel

- Feathered and bushy, with many branches
- Brown or olive in colour
- Turns green when taken from water

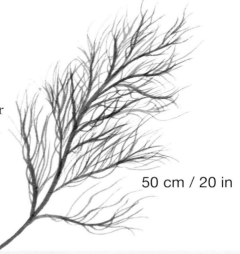

50 cm / 20 in

HABITAT	ZONE	TYPE
		Brown

Dulse

- Broad red leaves found in surf and on the beach
- Edible species, sold in food stores in Atlantic Canada

40 cm /16 in

HABITAT	ZONE	TYPE
		Red

Irish Moss

- Grows in clusters, with small leathery tufts
- Clings to rocks by holdfast at its base
- Reddish-purple colour lightens as it bleaches
- Harvested for commercial use

5 cm / 2 in

HABITAT	ZONE	TYPE
		Red

Purple Laver

- Very thin, slightly ruffled leaf
- Colour varies from green to purple
- Becomes black and brittle when dried

7 cm / 2.75 in

HABITAT   ZONE   TYPE
Red

Coral Weed

- Coral-like, with jointed branching
- Very hardy plant with holdfast for cementing to rocks

4 cm /1.5 in

HABITAT   ZONE   TYPE
Red

Marram Grass

- Long, thin green leaves with dried residual material at base
- Grows in large colonies
- Long, yellow flower grows on stiff spikelet

1 m / 36 in

HABITAT **ZONE** **FLOWERS**
July–Sept

American Dune Grass

- Grows in large areas mixed with other grasses
- Wide leaves grow erect
- Light brown flowers form clusters at top of stem

1.5 m / 54 in

HABITAT   **ZONE** **FLOWERS**
July–Sept

Bulrush

- Tall erect stems grow in dense groups
- Grows in brackish or fresh waters
- Flowers form reddish-brown clusters

120 cm / 60 in

HABITAT   ZONE   FLOWERS
in August

Common Cattail

- Clusters of long flat leaves
- Dark brown erect flower with protruding stalk
- Grows in wet areas

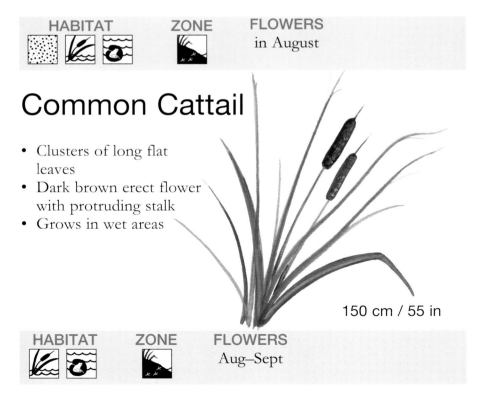

150 cm / 55 in

HABITAT   ZONE   FLOWERS
Aug–Sept

56

Seaside Spurrey

- Grows on higher areas of beaches
- Stems swell at ends with thick leaves and small white or pink flowers

15 cm / 8 in

HABITAT	ZONE	FLOWERS
		July–Sept

Seaside Iris

- Long spiked leaves spread out
- Grows in small groups among grasses in wet areas
- Also known as Blue Flag

30 cm / 16 in

HABITAT	ZONE	FLOWERS
		June–July

Eelgrass

- Aquatic grass-like plant
- Leaves seen flowing just below water's surface
- Small green flowers at base of leaf produce oval fruit

120 cm / 48 in

| HABITAT | ZONE | FLOWERS |

June–Sept

Samphire

- Succulent stem and branches, bright green in Spring
- Turns red-brown in late summer and fall
- Grows in dense colonies
- Also known as Glasswort and Marsh Greens

30 cm / 12 in

HABITAT   ZONE

Common Wild Rose

2 m / 10 ft

- Large bushes can have brown and green stems
- Small, green, toothed-edged leaves

HABITAT	ZONE	FLOWERS
		July–Aug

Wild Morning Glory

3 m / 36 in

- Vine-like with triangular leaves
- White or pink funnel-shaped flowers have 5 large petals

HABITAT	ZONE	FLOWERS
		June–Sept

Seaside Goldenrod

- Long, thick stems with leaves that broaden toward base of plant
- Yellow flowers cluster at main branch

60 cm / 24 in

HABITAT	ZONE	FLOWERS	
		July–Sept	2 m / 24 in

Beach Pea

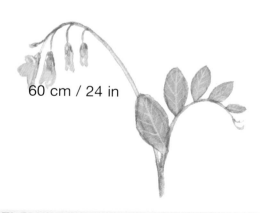

- Vine grows among grasses and bushes
- Pink or purple flowers form clusters on long stems

60 cm / 24 in

HABITAT	ZONE	FLOWERS
		June–Sept

Mayweed

- Grows in large populations
- Narrow leaves

15 cm / 6 in

HABITAT	ZONE	FLOWERS
		July–Sept

Dusty Miller

- Broad hairy leaves grow at base of large stem
- Cluster of yellow flowers at top of stem

30 cm / 12 in

HABITAT	ZONE	FLOWERS
		Aug–Oct

Sea Rocket

- Fleshy leaves and stems
- Rocket-shaped seeds
- Clustered pale lavender flowers
- Grows well above high tide mark

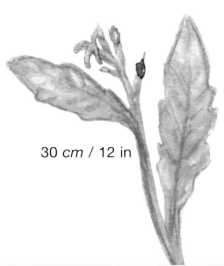

30 *cm* / 12 in

HABITAT	ZONE	FLOWERS
		July–Sept

Seaside Buttercup

- Small flowers with 5 petals grow singly or in clusters
- Broad rounded leaves on erect stem

15 cm / 6 in

HABITAT	ZONE	FLOWERS
		June–Sept

Roseroot

30 cm /12 in

- Fleshy, overlapping reddish leaves with toothed edge
- Thick stem, flowers clustered at top
- Flowers turn purple when going to seed

HABITAT	ZONE	FLOWERS
		June–July

Scotch Lovage

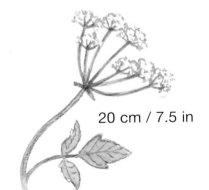

20 cm / 7.5 in

- Groups of three leaves, the center one largest
- Umbrella-like clusters of small white flowers

HABITAT	ZONE	FLOWERS
		July–Aug

Sea Lugwort

- Red and blue bell-shaped flowers cluster and droop at ends
- Thick broad leaves most dense at bottom
- Found well above tide line

70 cm / 28 in

HABITAT	ZONE	FLOWERS
		June–Aug

Foxberry

- Stem creeps along ground with branches standing erect
- White or pink bell-shaped flowers grow at top of stem
- Small red berries in fall

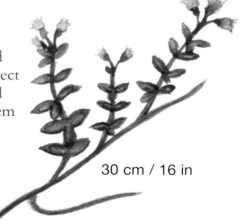

30 cm / 16 in

HABITAT	ZONE	FLOWERS
		June–July

Red Fox

120 cm / 44 in

- Trots, head to the ground sniffing for prey
- Omnivorous, feeds on crabs, small rodents and carrion, as well as berries in fall

1 Overall reddish-gold short hair

2 Dark and bushy tail with white tip

3 Black lower legs and paws

HABITAT   ZONE

Raccoon

STATUS
Common

- Forages at night but occasionally seen during daylight hours
- Walks with a slow waddle but can run fast
- Washes food before eating

100 cm / 38 in

HABITAT   ZONE

Ermine

- Moves quickly, close to the ground
- Dark coat turns white in winter

34 cm / 13 in

HABITAT	ZONE	STATUS
		Common

Meadow Jumping Mouse

- Jumps in long, fast leaps
- Out of imminent danger, will remain motionless until threat passes

26 cm / 10 in (including tail)

❶ Long tail and legs ❷ Brown overall with yellowish hints along sides ❸ Pink legs and feet

HABITAT	STATUS
	Common

Black Fly

- Flies silently
- Hovers, then lands, looking for a protected spot, such as under a collar, before biting

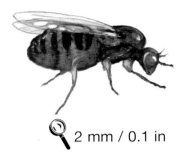

2 mm / 0.1 in

Deer Fly

- Circles target
- Bites and sucks blood from victim
- Leaves a red swelling

12 mm / 0.5 in

Horse Fly

- Buzzes loudly in flight
- Draws blood when it bites
- Distinguished from Deer Fly by larger head

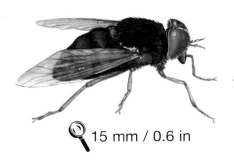

15 mm / 0.6 in

Yellow Jacket

- Delivers a painful sting
- Distinct yellow and black markings
- Folds brown wings compactly against body
- Nests underground or in hollow trees

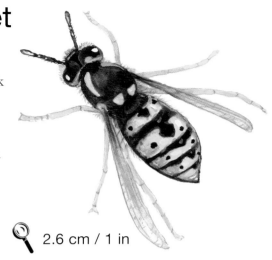

2.6 cm / 1 in

HABITAT   ZONE

Bumble Bee

- Not aggressive and rarely stings
- Furry with black and yellow markings
- Brown wings fold back over body

 15 mm / 0.6 in

HABITAT   ZONE

Crane Fly

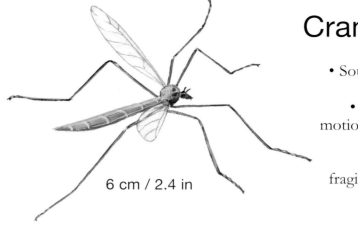

6 cm / 2.4 in

- Soundless and harmless
- Often seen motionless in the grass
- Long and fragile thin dark brown legs

HABITAT ZONE

Mosquito

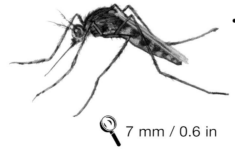

7 mm / 0.6 in

- High buzzing sound when flying
- Only females bite, drawing blood for egg laying
- Males and females live on plant nectar

HABITAT   ZONE

Wolf Spider

- Moves very quickly over rocks and around plants
- Often seen carrying a white ball of eggs on its back
- Small speckles on flat, hairy body

2 cm / 0.75 in

HABITAT

ZONE

Ladybird Beetle

- Small, rounded body with short black legs
- Yellow, orange or bright red wing covers feature black spots

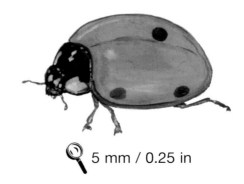

5 mm / 0.25 in

HABITAT

ZONE

Tiger Swallowtail

- Brilliant yellow with distinctive black stripes and blue patches
- Red tip and blue patches on tails

14 cm / 5.5 in

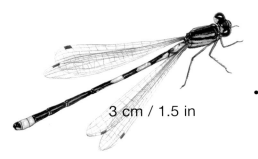

Damselfly

- Long, slender body is black with blue or green
- Large black eyes with blue spots at either sides of head

3 cm / 1.5 in

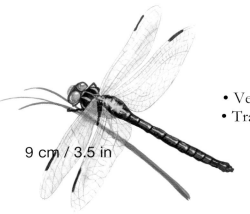

Dragonfly

- Very large with varying colours
- Transparent wings with various colour markings at ends
- Large bulging eyes at sides of head

9 cm / 3.5 in

Green Frog

12 cm / 4 in

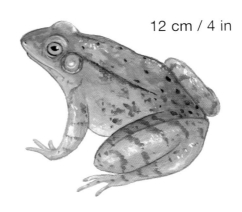

- Call is deep and twangy
- Lives near water

❶ Eardrum appears as large circle on side of head

❷ Back green with brown and bronze, yellow underside

❸ Ridges run down sides of back

HABITAT **ZONE** **STATUS**
Common

Northern Spring Peeper

3.5 cm / 1.2 in

- At daybreak and dusk in spring, chorus of repeated peeps, high-pitched and descending
- Migrates to small ponds after hibernation

❶ Large toe pads

❷ Very pale 'X' mark on back

❸ Various colours; mostly brown or grey on back and sides, yellow on underside

HABITAT **ZONE** **STATUS**
Common

Pickerel Frog

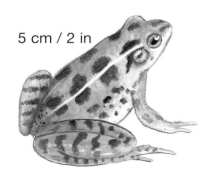

5 cm / 2 in

- Found near fresh water, along streams and lake shores
- Also seen in roadside areas and meadows
- Call is short, low-pitched snore

1 Irregular brown markings in rows

2 Yellow-brown with orange

HABITAT	ZONE	STATUS
		Common

Northern Leopard Frog

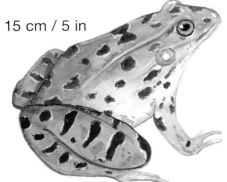

15 cm / 5 in

- In spring, male's call is a deep rattle
- Easily approached and will not jump until last second

1 Long legs and pointed snout

2 Black spots with white, underside spotted white

3 Pale strips run length of darker green body

HABITAT	ZONE	STATUS
		Common

Eastern American Toad

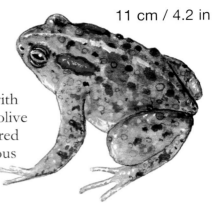

11 cm / 4.2 in

- Usually nocturnal
- Lives in moist areas by large insect populations

 Large with warts and spots of varying shades, mostly dark

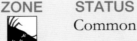 Brown with hints of olive or brick-red and various light colours

HABITAT **ZONE** **STATUS**
Common

Eastern Painted Turtle

- Sits motionless in small groups beside lakes and ponds
- Easily frightened
- Will leap into water and descend to bottom for short period

25.5 cm / 10 in

 HABITAT **ZONE** **STATUS**
Common

Maritime Garter Snake

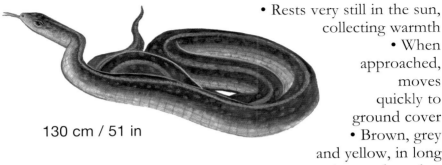

130 cm / 51 in

- Rests very still in the sun, collecting warmth
- When approached, moves quickly to ground cover
- Brown, grey and yellow, in long stripes and patches

HABITAT	ZONE	STATUS
		Common

Yellow-spotted Salamander

15 cm / 5 in

- Vary in colour from black to greyish-brown
- Occasionally spots are orange
- Remain under cover in daytime

HABITAT	ZONE

Short-billed Dowitcher

- Flies close to water's surface with quick wing beats
- Soft high-pitch call is *tu*, repeated several times

1 Back and wings speckled brown

2 Rust tint to neck, chest speckled black

3 Dark brown cap on head

4 Long dark beak and greenish legs

30 cm / 12 in

DID YOU KNOW?
In the spring, large flocks of dowitchers gather and feed by probing deeply in mud and sand.

HABITAT	ZONE	STATUS
		Common

Dunlin

- Very tame and easy to approach
- Call is *cheeerp* or *chit-lit*
- Steady, fast wing beats

1 Wings, like back, dull brown with white edging

2 Grey face with rust and black speckled crown

3 Distinct black patch on belly

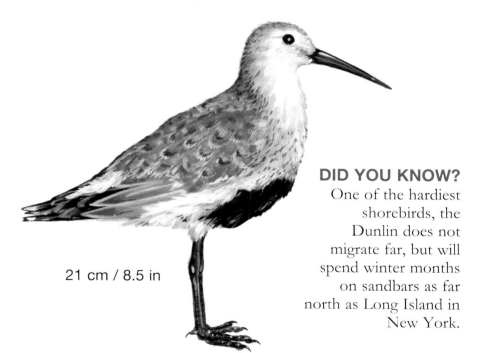

21 cm / 8.5 in

DID YOU KNOW?
One of the hardiest shorebirds, the Dunlin does not migrate far, but will spend winter months on sandbars as far north as Long Island in New York.

HABITAT	ZONE	STATUS
		Common

Great Black-backed Gull

- Dominates all other gulls
- Waits near other birds for opportunities to steal food
- Call is a very deep and guttural *keeeow*

1 Large, with black back and tops of wings

2 Yellow beak

3 White head, chest and belly

4 Underside of wings white, with black or grey wing tips

DID YOU KNOW?
This is the largest gull in the world.

76 cm / 30 in

STATUS
Common

HABITAT

ZONE

Herring Gull

- Loud calls include *kuk-kuk-kuk* and *yucca-yucca-yucca*
- Lowers head when calling
- Steady wing beats followed by extended gliding
- Dives for food at surface of water
- Scavenges behind fishing boats

1 Light grey back, wings grey with black tips

2 Yellow bill with red spot near tip of lower mandible

3 Feet and legs pink or yellowish

DID YOU KNOW?
The Herring Gull preys on nesting colonies of terns.

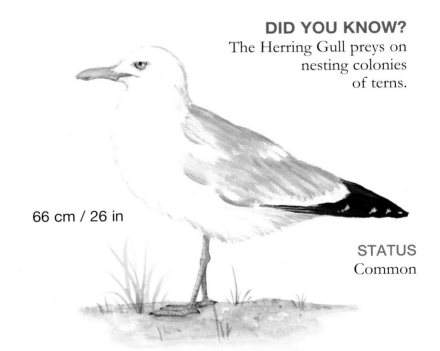

66 cm / 26 in

STATUS
Common

HABITAT

ZONE

Ring-billed Gull

- Short burst of wing beats followed by long stretch of gliding
- Loud *kaawk* and other calls

1 Distinct black band near tip of yellow bill

2 Yellow eye with pink or red ring around it

3 Black tips on tail and wings

DID YOU KNOW?
One of the most widespread gulls, the Ring-billed Gull is found from southern Canada to Cuba.

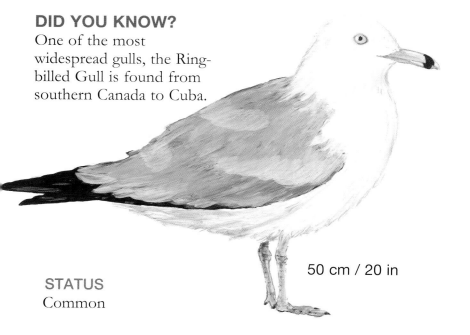

50 cm / 20 in

STATUS
Common

HABITAT   ZONE

Great Blue Heron

- Stands quite still in shallow waters
- When hunting, moves very slowly, then thrusts long beak into water, grabbing small fish or crabs
- Jumps upward, flies with big, slow wing beats

1 Overall grey-blue with black crest on top of head

2 Long neck with feathering toward chest

3 White patch under chin

4 Black patch between eye and bill

DID YOU KNOW?
The Great Blue Heron is distinctive in flight with a kinked neck and long legs dangling behind the wings.

130 cm / 52 in

STATUS
Common

HABITAT

ZONE

Belted Kingfisher

- Loud rattling call when perched and when taking flight
- Often perches on wires above freshwater lakes
- When fishing hovers, then dives head first into water

1 Pigeon-sized with large crested blue and black head

2 Blue and black overall, with distinct white collar

3 Wings black with white banding

4 Long, heavy black bill

DID YOU KNOW?
Belted Kingfishers teach their young to dive for food by catching and stunning a fish, then placing it on the surface of the water for the young birds to dive for.

33 cm / 13 in

HABITAT	ZONE	STATUS
		Common

Osprey

- In search of prey, hovers high over water for short periods
- Dives feet first from great heights into water, to capture fish
- Slow, steady wing beats
- Often seen carrying fish back to nest

1 Distinct black band running through eye

2 Tail grey with black banding

3 Back and top of wings black mixed with dark brown

DID YOU KNOW?
The Osprey's talon pads have short, sharp projections which help in holding prey upon capture.

61 cm / 24 in

HABITAT

ZONE

STATUS
Common

Bald Eagle

- Flies high above ground with long steady wing beat and occasional gliding
- Soars, riding thermals high above ground
- Often perches near water's edge, in dead or decaying trees

① Black overall with white head and tail feathers

② Thick yellow legs and talons with large black claws

③ Yellow eyes

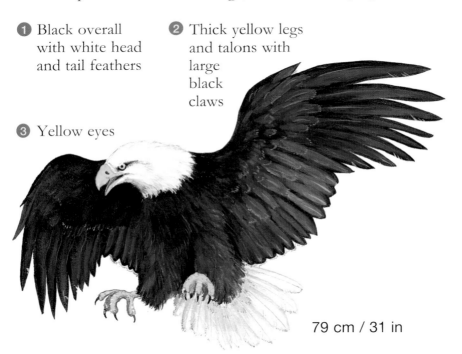

79 cm / 31 in

DID YOU KNOW?

Bald Eagles are an increasingly common sight throughout the year at feeding stations prepared by farmers.

HABITAT	ZONE	STATUS
		Common

Black-bellied Plover

- Found singly or in small groups
- Whistles *pee oo ee*
- Quick wing beats followed by glide

① Black breast and belly

② Pale grey speckled head, neck and crown

③ Black back with white speckles, white rump

④ In flight, bold white strip visible on underside of wing

33 cm / 13 in

DID YOU KNOW?

The largest plover is usually the first to fly away when approached, causing the other birds to take flight.

HABITAT   ZONE   STATUS
Common

Piping Plover

- Darts quickly then freezes
- Prods beak into sand at water line searching for worms and small insects
- In flight, wing beats are extremely fast
- Call is *peep peep peep*

1 Light greyish upper parts

2 White cheeks, chin, chest and belly

3 Distinct black band around neck, another across forehead

4 Bill is yellow or orange with black tip

DID YOU KNOW?

Piping plovers nest close to the shore in a depression in the sand, laying up to 4 sand-coloured eggs.

17 cm / 7 in

HABITAT	ZONE	STATUS
		Endangered

Semipalmated Plover

- Quick wing beats followed by gliding to ground
  - Whistles *chee-weee* in quick short notes
  - Slightly larger and darker than Piping Plover

1 Small white patch on fore-head with black banding above and below

2 Dark brown head, back and wings

3 White chin extends into white collar

4 Black collar extends around neck

20 cm / 8 in

DID YOU KNOW?
Like the Piping Plover, the Semipalmated Plover runs quickly along the beach stopping suddenly to feed or look around with a raised head.

HABITAT	ZONE	STATUS
		Common

Sanderling

- Quick wing beats when flying close to water's surface
- Calls *kip* in flight, chatters when feeding
- Runs quickly, right at water's edge

1 Bright brown and speckled head, back and breast

2 Black tail feathers tipped with white

3 Long bill is dark brown

4 Black feet and legs

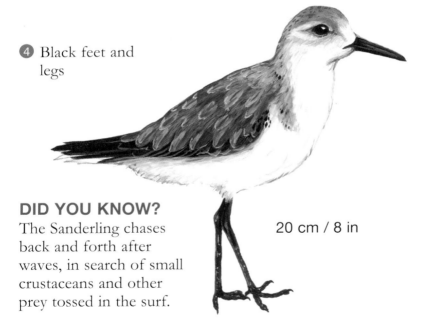

DID YOU KNOW?
The Sanderling chases back and forth after waves, in search of small crustaceans and other prey tossed in the surf.

20 cm / 8 in

HABITAT

ZONE

STATUS
Common

88

Purple Sandpiper

- Quick wing beats followed by gliding low to ground
- Calls *twheeet* and *twiiit*
- Usually in groups of about 50

1 Soft grey overall, with dark brown and rust spots

2 Chest fades to pale belly

3 Orange bill is slightly curved down, black at tip

4 Dark eyes with white eye rings

23 cm / 9 in

DID YOU KNOW?
This easily approached bird spends the winter in Atlantic Canada and breeds in summer in the Arctic.

HABITAT	ZONE	STATUS
		Common

Spotted Sandpiper

- Bobs tail up and down
- Quick wing beats followed by gliding close to ground
- When alarmed, whistles repeatedly or calls *peeeet-weeeet*

1 Grey-brown on head, back and wings

2 White eyebrow with black line running from bill to back

3 Long, dark orange bill

4 White chin, chest and belly speckled black

DID YOU KNOW?
It's bobbing motion has given this sandpiper the nickname Teeter-tail.

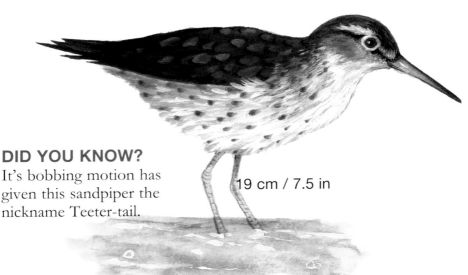

19 cm / 7.5 in

HABITAT	ZONE	STATUS
		Common

Common Tern

- Flies fast with quick wing beats
- From heights, dives into water after prey
- Attacks intruders in nesting grounds
- Call is *kip kip kip*, and *teeaar*
- Colonies threatened by introduced predators, such as rats

1 White overall with long black-tipped wings

2 Black cap

3 Orange-red bill with black tip

4 Forked white tail revealed in flight

40 cm / 16 in

DID YOU KNOW?
Fishing boats sometimes follow terns in order to find large schools of fish.

HABITAT	ZONE	STATUS
		Protected

91

Willet

- Flies low to ground with fast wing beats
- Very vocal
- Ring-like call similar to name "pill will willet," with quieter *kip kip kip*

1 Brownish-grey with white speckles

2 White at lower belly and rump

3 Long, heavy, pointed bill

4 Grey feet and legs

DID YOU KNOW?
The black and white pattern on the underside of the wings is the best feature for identifying the Willet.

38 cm / 15 in

HABITAT

ZONE

STATUS
Common

Greater Yellowlegs

- Flies low to ground or just above water with quick wing beats
- Nods head continuously when wading and searching for food

1 Speckled grey and white overall

2 Long bright yellow or orange legs

3 Long, straight, black bill

4 Short tail feathers with black banding

36 cm / 14 in

DID YOU KNOW?
In flight, the Greater Yellowleg extends its legs so that they dangle behind its wings.

HABITAT

ZONE

STATUS
Common

Double-crested Cormorant

- Black body with long snaky neck
- Floats submerged with head raised slightly above water

84 cm
33 in

Northern Gannet

- White overall with black-tipped wings
- Dives into water from a height of 20 m/60 feet

94 cm / 37 in

Red Knot

- Face, neck and chest are brick red in summer, grey in winter
- Usually spotted among thousands of other shorebirds in migration paths

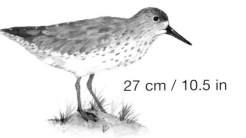

27 cm / 10.5 in

Common Loon

- Black, with distinctive white markings
- Warbling call heard early or late in the day, and at night

81 cm / 32 in

Canada Goose

- Brown overall, with long black neck and distinctive white chin
- Eats eelgrass and spends winters mostly in large flocks, floating just off the coast

63–114 cm / 25-45 in

HABITAT

Common Merganser

63 cm / 25 in

- Dark green crested head with orange toothed bill
- Diving duck, feeds on small fish

HABITAT

95

INDEX